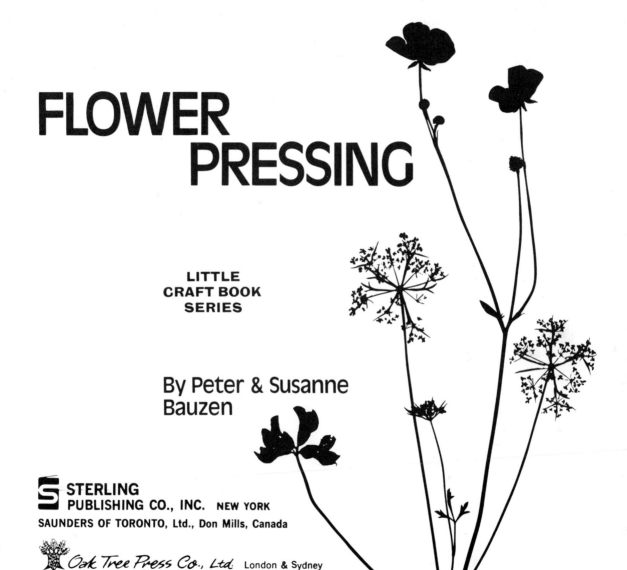

FLOWER PRESSING

LITTLE
CRAFT BOOK
SERIES

By Peter & Susanne
Bauzen

S STERLING
PUBLISHING CO., INC. NEW YORK
SAUNDERS OF TORONTO, Ltd., Don Mills, Canada

Oak Tree Press Co., Ltd. London & Sydney

Little Craft Book Series

Bargello Stitchery
Beads Plus Macramé
Big-Knot Macramé
Candle-Making
Cellophane Creations
Coloring Papers
Corrugated Carton Crafting
Creating Silver Jewelry with Beads
Creating with Beads
Creating with Burlap
Creating with Flexible Foam
Enamel without Heat
Felt Crafting
Flower Pressing
Ideas for Collage
Lacquer and Crackle

Macramé
Making Paper Flowers
Making Shell Flowers
Masks
Metal and Wire Sculpture
Model Boat Building
Nail Sculpture
Needlepoint Simplified
Off-Loom Weaving
Potato Printing
Puppet-Making
Repoussage
Scissorscraft
Scrimshaw
Sewing without a Pattern
Tole Painting

Whittling and Wood Carving

Originally published by Verlag Frech, Stuttgart-Botnang, Germany, © 1968, under the title "Gepresste Blumen"

Translated by Paul Kuttner

Adapted by Jane Lassner

Second Printing, 1972
Copyright © 1972 by Sterling Publishing Co., Inc.
419 Park Avenue South, New York, N.Y. 10016
Simultaneously published and Copyright © 1972 in Canada
by Saunders of Toronto, Ltd., Don Mills, Ontario
British edition published by Oak Tree Press Co., Ltd., Nassau, Bahamas
Distributed in Australia by Oak Tree Press Co., Ltd.,
P.O. Box 34, Brickfield Hill, Sydney 2000, N.S.W.
Distributed in the United Kingdom and elsewhere in the British Commonwealth
by Ward Lock Ltd., 116 Baker Street, London W 1
Library of Congress Catalog Card No.: 77 167661
ISBN 0-8069-5186 9   UK 7061 2326 3
5187 7

Contents

Before You Begin 4

Pressing and Preserving the Flowers 5
  Keeping the Flowers' Color

Plants under Glass 9
  Plant Flowers on Your Wall . . . Serving Cart or Table Top . . . Serving Trays

Pressed Flowers under Plastic Film 15
  Eyeglass Case . . . Place Mats and Coasters . . . Book Cover . . . Lamp Shade . . . Flowered
  Stationery . . . Napkin Holder . . . Matchbox Cover

Protecting Plants with Lacquer 24
  Book Ends . . . Wall Decorations . . . Jewelry of Flowers and Wood . . . Fibreglass Lamp Shade

Printing with Plants 31
  Covering a Photo Album . . . Writing Portfolio

Color Plates . . . . facing 36-37

Flowers and Leaves as Photographic Stencils 37

Embedding Plants in Polyester Resin 41

Index 48

Before You Begin

You can preserve hundreds of nature's plants and flowers by pressing the moisture out of them. Wherever you go in the country—in meadows, woods, along lakes or the banks of streams, by the sea, up hills or a mountain slope—you will find a great variety of flowers, grasses, leaves and plants. Even if you do not live near open country, your local florist can provide you with a large assortment of flowers and greenery. Once you begin selecting plants for pressing, you will notice many different kinds that you never really observed before.

For centuries, nature's admirers have pressed flowers, hoping to retain the beautiful colors and shapes. But all too often the colors faded or the shapes were distorted, because of incorrect methods of pressing. Even if the flower was successfully pressed, it soon crumbled or was lost with a mass of other souvenirs. To turn your flowers into a permanent memory, use them for decoration on any one of a dozen places. The ideas in this book are just a few suggestions; once you learn the correct way to treat your flowers, you can use them on almost any surface you see!

If you gather the plants yourself, plan to do it in the middle of the morning or in the middle or late afternoon on dry, sunny days. Avoid collecting plants early in the morning when there is still dew on them and in wet weather. Flowers cut at high noon on a hot day wither very quickly.

Most important, select only the most perfect flowers. Choose those which have blossomed very recently so the leaves do not shed. Make sure that the stem, petals and leaves have not been damaged by insects.

Cut the flowers sharply with a knife or a pair of scissors and place them carefully into a plastic bag, then into a large basket, so you do not crush them on your way home. Never tear a plant out by the roots or injure nearby bushes or trees. And be sure to observe local laws and courtesies: never cut flowers in a national park, for example, or on private property.

Pressing and Preserving the Flowers

If you collect flowers that wither quite rapidly, or if you are quite a distance from home, prepare a collector's press so you can begin drying the flowers while you are still in the country. You need two pieces of sturdy cardboard, two lengths of ribbon, and blotting paper, newsprint or a newspaper. The press should be large enough to hold the cut plants, but not so big that it becomes a chore to carry. A popular size is 8″ × 12″.

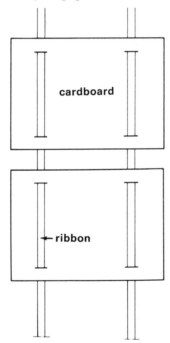

Illus. 1. A collector's press made of cardboard and ribbon should be the first piece of equipment for this craft. Take the press with you when you gather flowers.

Make four cuts into the corners of each piece of cardboard with a sharp pointed knife, and pull a ribbon through each set of four (see Illus. 1). Cut a piece of blotting paper the same dimensions as one cardboard and place it between the cardboard layers.

When you put the flowers inside the press, do not place them too close together. Arrange each flower carefully on the blotting paper so that no two flowers touch. The blossoms and leaves should lie flat, without any folds, curls, or creases.

Place flowers that are the same thickness next to each other so that they dry with the same amount of pressure. If flowers of different thicknesses lie side by side, they are not in even contact with the blotting paper and cannot dry completely. If thick flowers prevent thin leaves from being pressed firmly against the blotting paper, the thin leaves will curl and discolor as they dry without pressure.

After you have covered the blotting paper with flowers, place a few sheets of newspaper on them. Then gather more flowers of uniform thickness and arrange them on this layer of newspaper. The important thing is to arrange the thinner, delicate flowers on one layer and the thicker, sturdier ones on another so the flowers dry evenly.

When you have gathered as many flowers as you want, tighten the ribbons of your handmade flower press with enough pressure to start the drying process right away. At home, immediately add more newspaper between the layers of flowers. Place some heavy books on top of the press to increase the pressure, and after a few days,

Illus. 2. To press a flower with a thick center, place the blossom on blotting paper. Put another piece with a hole the same size as the center above the flower. Now all parts of the flower are level.

remove the books and replace the newspaper with fresh sheets. Try not to move any petals or leaves.

The time required to press the flowers varies with the type of flower, the temperature and humidity in the air, and the season of year. It is better to leave the flowers in the press too long, of course, rather than not long enough. Some flowers are sensitive to only a slight touch when they are in a half-dried state, so control your curiosity and leave the flowers in the press as long as possible.

If you are pressing a flower with thin petals but a thick center—like a daisy—you have a problem: how do you apply enough pressure to the delicate petals without crushing the center? Cut a hole about as big as the center of the daisy out of a piece of blotting paper, and place this holed piece on top of the flower. Add more holed blotting paper until the petal section of the flower is the same height as the center. Cover the entire set-up with a solid piece of blotting paper. When you apply the press and a heavy book, the pressure on all parts of the flower will be uniform.

Keeping the Flowers' Colors

Sometimes in spite of your careful precautions, pressed plants turn brown, either during the drying process or after you remove them from the press. Usually these plants did not dry fast enough, and so they withered before all the moisture was drawn out of them. Be careful to press the flowers as hard and long as possible—at least several days, and at best, several weeks.

After exposure to the air, some dried flowers lose their color and become transparent, or at least considerably faded compared to their original vibrant hues. The best and surest method to restore faded colors is to paint the plants with water colors after they have dried. On your first try, the water color may run off the dried plants without adhering at all. To avoid this, place a drop of detergent on your paintbrush and mix the detergent with the water color. Then paint as usual. If a plant is particularly water-repellent, add more detergent so the water color adheres. After painting the natural colors back on the blossoms, stem and leaves, set the pressed flowers aside to dry in the open air. If you pressed them thoroughly, they will not absorb the paint's moisture, just the pigment.

If thin, fragile petals become transparent when dry, painting them restores their color but does

Illus. 3. To restore lost colors to pressed flowers, paint them with water colors.

not make them sturdier. So that you can handle fragile petals, glue the blossoms to a sheet of paper which is the same color as the petals. Put some clear all-purpose glue on the paper and gently lay the plant on top of it. Spread the glue under the flower with a pin or toothpick and lightly rub off any excess glue around the petals. After the glue dries, if you do not want any paper around the blossom, cut around it with a pair of sharp scissors, going into every fine line and division of the petals. The paper's color will show through the transparent dried blossom.

Illus. 4. For both color and strength, glue pressed flowers to construction paper. Trim close to the flowers.

Plants under Glass

Plant Flowers on Your Wall

Now that you know how to press flowers, you may be wondering what to do with them. One of the simplest and prettiest projects you can make is a framed arrangement to hang on your wall. You need a piece of cardboard for the backing of the picture, a piece of construction paper the same size in an attractive color that either contrasts or harmonizes with the colors of the flowers, a pane of glass, and a picture frame. You also need the pressed flowers which you have chosen for the composition, and clear all-purpose glue for attaching them to the construction paper background. If you want to make a realistic hanging, attach real butterfly wings and paper butterfly bodies. Their colors and shiny texture make the arrangement look truly natural.

Choose large flowers for a wall decoration so they show up across the room. Large flowers usually have thick, harder stems, however, and you must make these narrower before you glue them to the paper backing so the glass can lie flat on top of them. Carefully remove the back side of the stem with a single-edge razor blade or a sharp knife. When you lay the glass on top of the almost-flat arrangement, it lies evenly on the paper background.

Before you glue anything, place all the flowers on the paper and analyze the arrangement, both from close up and at a distance. Notice the color, size, texture and species of flowers as you arrange them, and add the butterflies to highlight the flowers.

Illus. 5. Arrange the flowers on paper before you glue them down. Spread a thin layer of glue on the back of each flower with a toothpick.

9

To glue each piece to the paper, first put a few drops of glue behind the fattest part of the flower—most likely the stem or some thick leaves—and then draw some glue to the thinner areas with a pin or toothpick. When the glue has dried, check all pieces of the composition to see that they are firmly attached to the paper background.

There are several types of wire hooks to hold the glass, cardboard and construction paper together. Some grasp the layers at the top and have an extra loop for hanging from the wall, while others are made to hold the layers at the bottom to prevent them from slipping. Illus. 7 shows a few varieties; your hardware store has several additional styles. If you want to frame the entire composition, you do not need these hooks. Take the mounted flowers to a professional framer or buy a picture frame and frame the composition yourself. Hooks for hanging are already on the backs of most frames.

Illus. 6. A wall decoration, made of pressed flowers and butterflies glued to paper, then covered with a sheet of glass.

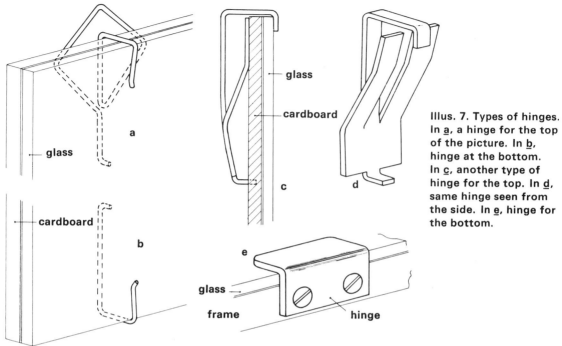

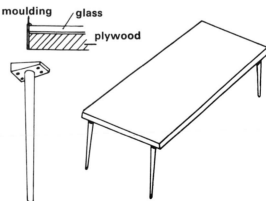

glass

cardboard

a

glass

cardboard

b

glass

frame

e

hinge

c

d

Illus. 7. Types of hinges. In <u>a</u>, a hinge for the top of the picture. In <u>b</u>, hinge at the bottom. In <u>c</u>, another type of hinge for the top. In <u>d</u>, same hinge seen from the side. In <u>e</u>, hinge for the bottom.

Serving Cart or Table Top

While wall hangings are attractive in your own home and as gifts, a serving cart or coffee table is a project that you can admire while using. If you have a cart or table with a removable glass top, you are in luck: just carefully lift the glass and glue a piece of smooth paper to the top. Arrange the flowers on this surface, replace the glass, and fill in the border around the edge of the glass with glue to protect the flowers underneath from spills and moisture.

If you are more ambitious, make a coffee table yourself. Buy a plywood board or a piece of

moulding   glass

plywood

Illus. 8. To make your own table, assemble these parts.

pressedboard about ½" thick of the size you want for the finished table—probably no smaller than 12" × 24". Lay a piece of good paper—rice paper, perhaps, or any other which is attractive and adds a fine look—on the board. Attach flowers to the paper as you did for the wall hanging. Remember to use only flowers that are of a uniform thickness or else slice the stems, so the glass can lie flat.

Lay a piece of glass in the proper size on top of the board (the store where you bought the glass will cut it for you). Glue or tack plastic or aluminium moulding around the edge of the board to seal it against dust and moisture and to hold the glass securely to the wood.

Carefully turn the board over and lay it on a soft surface. Now screw legs through flanges to the bottom. You can buy pre-cut, finished legs with flanges from a carpenter; they will probably be more level than any you could make at home. Attach one leg to each corner with screws or nails. Turn the table right side up again and give the glass a final polish. Perfect for a sunny room, your flowered coffee table will last indefinitely.

Illus. 9. Decorate a store-bought serving cart with flowers under the glass top.

12

Serving Trays

If you have a few pressed flowers that you want to use on a small project, a round serving tray might be just the thing. The glass surface is easy to clean, and the flowers under the glass add a decorative note to an ordinary household item. You attach the flowers the same way basically as on the serving cart and coffee table, but the tray's small size makes it easier to work on.

There are several kinds of bases you might use for the tray. The lids of large tin containers are ideal, since they already have a "lip" of metal which will seal the glass around the sides. If a metal lid is not available, use a round piece of plywood or board and add an extra piece of aluminium around the outside edge.

Attach a piece of good paper to the tray's base and glue the flowers to the paper. Remember that leaves, weeds, grasses and even seeds and roots can make just as attractive an arrangement as the colorful petals of a flower do. When the glue under the dried arrangement has set, carefully place the glass on top of the wood or metal circle.

13

Illus. 11. A wooden tray with glass to protect it can be brightened with pressed flowers.

If the base already has a lip around the outside, put clear-drying glue which adheres to glass in the small space between the lip and the glass, to protect the flowers from moisture and to keep the glass from falling out. If there is no lip around the base, make one of a flexible metal and glue it to the base and glass.

You might prefer to use clear Plexiglas instead of glass; it is lighter than glass and less likely to break if dropped. Buy Plexiglas from a plastics supplier, who will cut it to the proper size, or cut it yourself with a fret saw after outlining the circle. If there are any ragged or uneven edges, file them off with fine sandpaper. Use the Plexiglas just as you would glass: remember to add clear-drying glue in the space between the Plexiglas and the metal lip.

Pressed Flowers under Plastic Film

Suppose you have collected, pressed and dried a beautiful arrangement of flowers, but want to use the plants in a project that you can carry around with you? Even if you do not seal your flowers under glass, you can still protect them—just place transparent plastic film over the arrangement. The flowers are permanently fixed, the plastic is as clear as glass, and the project—no matter what it is—can be moved, carried around, and used often.

Practice on small projects while you learn to work with plastic film, as it is sometimes tricky to manipulate. There are two kinds: plastic film that is self-adhesive, and plastic film that is not. The self-adhesive kind has two layers to it; one layer is the film itself, and the other layer is a backing which protects the film until it is peeled off. The second type of film requires a special solvent to make it stick, or sometimes a cool iron to melt the invisible backing substance. The craft supply store where you buy the film will tell you what material you need to make that type of film adhere.

Eyeglass Case

A small cloth eyeglass case is easy to make: use the glasses as a rough pattern and cut around them on two thicknesses of fabric. Before you sew the two pieces together, decorate one side with pressed flowers. Glue the flowers to the fabric backing in just a few main places. Now you are ready to attach the plastic film.

If you are using self-adhesive film, cut a piece about $\frac{1}{2}''$ larger all around than the eyeglass case. Carefully peel the backing layer from the film at one side only, and place the film on the cloth exactly where it belongs. Once the flowers touch the film, they are stuck there, so avoid touching the film to places it does not belong.

As you peel the backing away, smooth the film on the cloth with your hand or a rolled-up rag, to get rid of air pockets and make the film as smooth as possible. Because air pockets are not uncommon even in small areas, avoid using plastic film on large areas, as sometimes a bumpy, unattractive surface results.

Illus. 12. Place dried flowers on cloth; then cover with plastic film. Lace together for an eyeglass case.

Illus. 13. Decorate a place mat with flowers and cover with protective plastic film.

When the cloth is decorated and covered with plastic, attach the two pieces together. One attractive way is to punch holes around the outside edges of both pieces of fabric (through the film also, of course). Then line up the holes of the two pieces together, and sew with an overcast stitch. You can use an attractive thread or leather thongs for the stitching. You will be reminded of your creative energies with flowers every time you reach for your glasses!

Place Mats and Coasters

These are ideal for decorating with flowers and covering with plastic. Since the surface of a mat or coaster is frequently subjected to spills and lots of scrubbing, use a sturdy plastic both on top of the flowers and under the cardboard or felt backing. Use thin flowers and leaves, since the mat should be flat so dishes do not spill.

First cut out cardboard or felt in the size and shape you want the mat or coaster to be. If you are making a set, cut all the pieces at once, so they are identical. Arrange the flowers or leaves on the surface you are going to cover, and fasten them there with clear-drying glue. Now you can attach the plastic film, first on the front side and then on the back. Trim any excess plastic from the sides, punch holes around the outside edge, and insert your chosen lacing—yarn, thread, cord, leather, nylon, plastic or whatever—around and around through the holes. Use colorful fall leaves for your mats for a seasonal meal.

Book Cover

To protect the cover of your book as you carry it with you, make a floral book cover the same way you made an eyeglass case. Before you attach the flowers to the cloth, however, glue the cloth to two sheets of cardboard, and attach a narrow elastic strip at the top and bottom of each cardboard, which you will later slip over the book's covers.

Any arrangement of flowers will look attractive on a wide expanse of dark fabric; just be sure to place them carefully. First glue the flowers to the fabric as usual. Now carefully place the plastic film on top of all the layers, smoothing it from the middle to the edges to get rid of air bubbles. Add lacing around the outside as you did on the eyeglass case, for a finished edge. With a plastic film cover for protection, you can carry this book in any weather.

Lamp Shade

The projects so far have involved covering flat surfaces, first with flowers and then with plastic film. A lamp shade is curved, but it is really no trickier to decorate than the place mat or book cover. And if you just attach flowers to an old lamp shade, you can have a bright design almost as quickly as you turn on the light.

Carefully disassemble an old shade, reserving the wire at the top and bottom so you can use it

Illus. 14. Glue cloth over two pieces of cardboard; then add flowers and plastic film for a book cover.

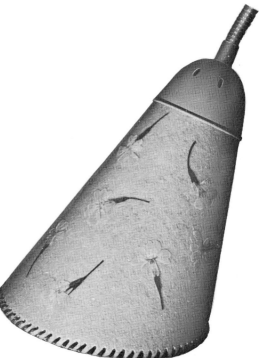

Illus. 15. Take apart an old lamp shade and glue pressed flowers to it. Save the wire top and bottom so you can re-assemble it.

again when you put the shade back together. If you are simply recovering a good shade, spread the pressed flowers on the flattened shade and glue them there. Then cover the shade with plastic film. Gently curl the shade back to the size and shape it was before. To fasten the shade in a cylinder or cone shape, either glue one edge of it on top of itself, or lace the edges together with heavy thread, cord, leather or plastic strips.

The wire at the top and bottom of the shade is there to help the shade maintain its shape and to prevent its curling. When you curl the shade back to its original size, it should fit snugly around the wire again (some shades fit over the wire, in which case the newly decorated shade will do the same). Again, you can glue the wire to the shade, or lace it with the same material you used for the side of the shade. Replace the lamp shade on the lamp, and you have a handsome ornament for your room.

Illus. 16. The finished lamp shade, fitted to the wire frame and decorated with lacing.

18

While it is always important to dry the flowers completely, it is vital to do so when you use the flowers on a lamp shade. The heat from the electric light will dry the flowers out rapidly if they are not already dry, and rapid drying causes color changes. After you have taken the time to prepare an attractive lamp shade, you do not want brown, straw-like flowers!

Flowered Stationery

For a gift or for yourself, hand-decorated stationery provides a delightful background for a greeting. And you can make the stationery in any size—small, for note paper, or large, for long, newsy letters.

Place cards for a party always add a thoughtful touch that shows how well you planned. First ink in the names on plain white cards—any size is good, but 3″×2″ is standard. If you can make fancy lettering, this adds appeal to the cards, but of course even the plainest printing will be appreciated. When the ink is dry, attach the flowers in one corner of the card with clear-drying all-purpose glue. Spread the glue along the thinner parts of the flower with a toothpick or pin, and set the cards aside to dry.

Since place cards are not handled too much—they are really made only to be admired—you may not want to cover the cards with plastic film. If you think your guests will want to keep their cards, however (and if you designed them artistically, they probably will), attach some film over the front of the card. This project would be a good one to practice on using the second kind of film, the kind that needs either solvent or heat to adhere. Rub the solvent on the film for as long

as the manufacturer directs, and then put the cards face down on the film. You can either trim the film along the edges of the card, or fold the film along the edges so it meets in the middle of the wrong side of the card. Press the film together so it sticks; then trim any extra.

Make greeting cards and writing paper in basically the same way: glue the flowers to the paper; then cover just the flowers with film. For a special touch on the front of a card, first attach flowers to a dark piece of paper and cover it all with film. Then glue this paper to a larger piece of white stock, folded in half. Birthday greetings,

Illus. 17. Neatly print guests' names on cards; then add flowers and cover with film.

19

get-well wishes, or any sort of salutation goes well on this card.

For a unique gift, make several sheets of decorated stationery and put them in a flower-covered box. Since the box will probably be used long after the stationery is gone, cover it carefully with heavy plastic film (see Illus. 24).

Napkin Holder

Since anything of metal, plastic, wood, cardboard or paper can be covered with pressed flowers and plastic film, there are probably hundreds of items you are dying to get your hands on to liven up. How about that plain paper-napkin holder that stays in the kitchen because it's too ordinary to be used for company meals? If

Illus. 18. Make a stationery assortment with a different flower on each sheet. Decorate the box top too.

you want to keep the present holder in the kitchen, you can make another napkin holder from a few pieces of cardboard and a small piece of wood, and add flowers and greenery for a refreshing decoration.

Cut a piece of stiff cardboard in a simple geometric design that is symmetrical at both ends— a half-circle, rectangle, triangle or more elaborate shape. Leaving a space about 1″ wide in the middle of the cardboard, score the board on either side of the 1″. Bend the cardboard up along the score lines. The 1″-area is the base of the holder, while the sides support the napkins.

To make the holder sturdier and prevent it from toppling over, add a piece of wood about ½″ thick to the cardboard base. Smooth it with sandpaper or a plane to avoid splinters; then put the wood

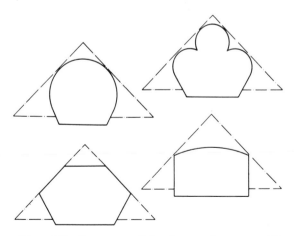

Illus. 20. Some possible shapes for a napkin holder.

21

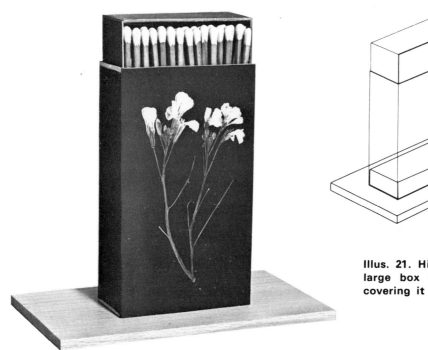

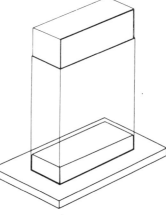

Illus. 21. Hide the advertising on a large box of kitchen matches by covering it with paint, flowers and film.

inside the cardboard and glue it there. Paint all parts of the holder an attractive but neutral color that makes a good background for the flowers.

Glue flowers to the holder as usual, and cover the cardboard with plastic film. Even as mechanical a motion as reaching for a napkin now has a bit of beauty!

Matchbox Cover

Make an attractive holder for a large box of kitchen or fireplace matches, so you never have to hunt for them again. First smooth a piece of wood with sandpaper; this is the base of the holder. Carefully trim a small block of wood until it is slightly smaller all round than the cover of the matchbox. Glue this wood piece to the base.

If the matchbox cover has advertisements or lettering on it, paint it with an attractive color. Glue small flowers to the front and cover them with plastic film. Remember to leave the striking edge of the matchbox cover free of paint, flowers and film.

Place the cover on top of the small wood block and glue it there. Now slide the inner box which holds the matches into the cover. Because of the wood block underneath, the box will not slide down all the way. Rather, the match heads will peek over the edge of the cover, reminding you of your clever craftsmanship every time you look their way.

Protecting Plants with Lacquer

For wooden objects which could use extra gloss as well as decorative flowers, transparent lacquer does double duty: it protects and fastens the flowers, at the same time that it protects and adds shine to the wood. Some lacquers are water-proof when dry; this type would be appropriate for trays, the backs of hairbrushes or anything which might get wet.

When you buy wood for decorating with flowers and lacquer, look at the texture and grain. Try to find an attractive surface, but not so unusual that it detracts from the flowers. Smooth all parts of the wood with fine sandpaper or emery paper, and remove the fine dust from the surface.

Apply a thin layer of lacquer to the wood with a brush, let it dry, and smooth the surface again with sandpaper. Be sure to keep your brush from hardening by keeping it in a can of lacquer remover. Now apply a second coat of lacquer. Spread the flowers on the wet surface, and press them gently with the brush so they stay put. When this lacquer layer is dry, cover everything with another coat. If parts of the plant protrude from the wood surface, apply a thick coat of lacquer at those places so the flower does not peel or rub off.

Book Ends

For a pair of book ends for a den or study, cut two pieces of wood into identical shapes. Sand them smooth; then either screw or glue a piece of aluminium bent into a right angle to the bottom for a base (see Illus. 23). Glue some felt or foam rubber to the bottom of the aluminium to protect your furniture from scratches.

Now apply a coat of lacquer to the wood and let it dry. Sand it. Apply a second coat, and while it is still wet, gently place the flowers on top. Add

Illus. 22. Buy or make a pair of bookends. Using lacquer as glue, attach pressed flowers to the ends.

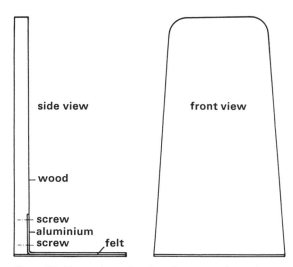

side view

front view

wood

screw
aluminium
screw   felt

Illus. 23. To make a bookend, cut and sand an attractive piece of wood. Before you add flowers, attach a piece of aluminium to the bottom, and some felt under that to prevent scratches.

Illus. 24. Even an empty canister, from a tin of coffee or cookies, becomes an attractive decoration when flowers are lacquered to it.

a third coat to protect the flowers. Depending on the thickness of the wood, these book ends can support as much weight as any pair you might buy.

Wall Decorations

Because it is so easy to attach flowers to wood with lacquer as the glue, you might be tempted to make a large project to hang on the wall. And why not? A large project is just as easy to make as a small one. A wall decoration can be as big or as little as you like, of course; just be sure that the wood you choose as a background is evenly and attractively grained, and not warped.

Sand and polish the wood until it is as smooth as can be. Apply one coat of clear lacquer; sand again; then apply a second coat and lay the flowers

Illus. 25. A decoration
for your wall, made from
a curved piece of wood
with pressed flowers
lacquered to it.

in this wet layer. For a more three-dimensional collage, use sturdy, thick grasses and flowers. Greenery with very thick stems absorbs a lot of lacquer and must be covered again and again until the lacquer dries on the surface of the stem. While applying many layers takes time, it makes dusting the wall decoration easier later.

If you apply many coats of lacquer to one side of a thin wood board, it may warp in one direction. To prevent this, lacquer the back of the board also.

Jewelry of Flowers and Wood

Necklaces, pins and fancy hair ornaments are small, easy-to-make gift ideas that will be worn and appreciated for years to come. Buy the most beautifully grained wood you can find for this jewelry, and shape and sand it until it is attractive by itself. Attach small flowers with lacquer, as described above, and then attach jewelry "findings" to the back of the wood. Findings are the pins, clasps, loops, and hooks that turn the wood into a piece of jewelry. Buy them at a craft or hobby shop.

Fibreglass Lamp Shade

While wood is an attractive and easy surface to cover with lacquer, fibreglass is even easier, since it requires no sanding or smoothing. Just be sure you use a clear-drying lacquer, not the yellowish kind. Test your lacquer on a small piece of fibreglass for a bookmark before you begin a large project.

When you are acquainted with the type of lacquer you are using and how it adheres to the fibreglass, you are ready to make your own lamp shade. The shade in Illus. 30, for which instruc-

Illus. 26. Make a pendant or pin from a scrap piece of wood. Just attach the appropriate jewelry findings.

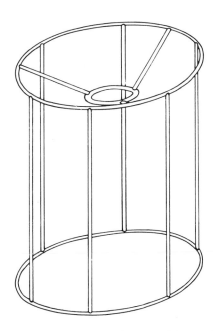

Illus. 27. The wire frame of a round lamp shade is shaped like this.

Illus. 28. Cut fibreglass sheets to fit around the shade's frame. Lay the flowers on each sheet side by side.

tions are given here, is going to cover a round hanging lamp. Carefully cut the old shade off the round metal structure that you are going to recover and use the old shade as a pattern for the fibreglass. Cut the fibreglass into sheets to fit around the steel structure. Assemble the sheets together while you curve them into a cylinder. Curve the shade to fit tightly over the metal, so it needs adhesive only at its seams, not at the top or bottom.

Once the fibreglass is curved around the base of the shade, apply a coat of lacquer and let it dry. Apply a second coat; then gently lay the flowers, leaves and grasses on the shade. Since the lacquer must be applied when the lamp lies horizontal, to prevent dripping, you can only decorate those few panels which face up at one time. This takes longer than attaching all the flowers at once, but the perfect results are well worth the extra minutes.

Illus. 29. Lacquer the flowers to the fibreglass sheets, allowing each panel to dry before you turn the shade.

Illus. 30. A tall lamp shade seems even taller with the addition of long grasses.

Illus. 31. A delicate pressed fern decorates the top of a wood box. The lacquer adds gloss to the wood as it makes the fern adhere.

Printing with Plants

Many plants and especially leaves can be used as stamps for printing. While they are usually not durable enough to print hundreds of copies, with care they can last through a dozen or so prints—enough for a box of stationery or a motif on wrapping paper. Some fragile plants break or curl after only a few uses, but this just makes the successful prints more valuable.

Covering a Photo Album

Albums which hold family pictures are often in need of new covers, since frequent handling makes the old ones fall apart quickly. A simple and inexpensive way to cover an album—or any scrapbook or loosely bound volume—is to attach hand-decorated paper to the top of the old cover. In Illus. 32, the new cover is paper printed with a scattered design of a delicately grained leaf.

Choose a thick, durable paper cut to the proper size. For the album in Illus. 32, only a small amount of paper was needed, since the binding was covered with tape. Make a few test patterns with the leaf you plan to use to find out exactly how much ink or paint you should apply for the best results. Use either India ink or printer's ink.

Illus. 32. Ink one side of a leaf and press it on paper. Use the paper for anything—perhaps to cover a photo album.

31

Give one side of the leaf an even coat of ink with a brush, and turn it over so the inked side is against the paper. Cover the leaf with some absorbent paper. Using your hand or a rolled handkerchief, rub the paper and leaf with even strokes. Then remove the paper, and finally the leaf carefully.

If some parts of the leaf did not print as darkly as others on the paper, do *not* re-ink the leaf and attempt to place it on top of the first design. At best, you will produce a fuzzy double image, since it is almost impossible to place the leaf in exactly the right spot. To fill in a faint part of the print, dip a thin brush into the ink and carefully and lightly go over the spot on the paper.

When the paper is printed with the design you want, set it aside to dry for a few hours. Fold and trim it to fit around the covers of the album or book you are covering; then glue it in place. For greater protection, cover the paper with durable plastic film.

Illus. 34. Quickly and evenly press the painted side of the flower to the paper. Lift it, and the pattern remains.

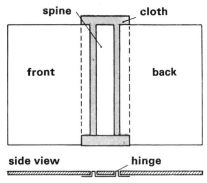

Illus. 35. Place two pieces of cardboard on a strip of cloth to begin a writing portfolio.

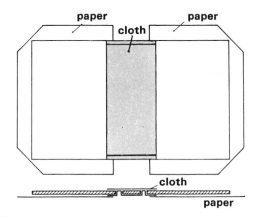

Illus. 36. Cover the front of the cardboard with decorated paper and glue a strip of cloth to the inside of the spine.

Writing Portfolio

For a gift that you make from scratch, a writing portfolio is attractive and not at all difficult. It is sure to be appreciated by anyone who writes letters, and its decorative cover of printed flowers will remind the owner of the outdoors while he writes letters indoors.

Use two sturdy pieces of chipboard (layered cardboard), longer and wider than standard sheets of stationery. For the spine of the portfolio, use a strip of cardboard about 1″ wide. Place a piece of cloth about 3″ wide flat on your work-table and glue the cardboard spine in the middle of this. Glue the chipboard to the cloth on each side of the cardboard, leaving about ½″ between the edges of the spine and the chipboard. Fold the ends of the cloth in and cover the inside of the spine with another piece of cloth.

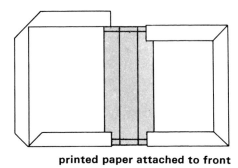

printed paper attached to front

Illus. 37. Neatly fold and glue the paper to the inside of the cardboard covers.

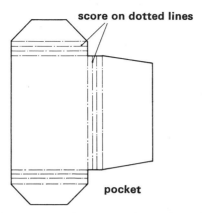

score on dotted lines

pocket

Illus. 38. To make a pocket, cut a sheet of sturdy
paper in this shape. Score along the dotted lines
shown here.

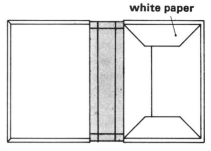

white paper

Illus. 39. Glue the pocket to one side of the
portfolio, and a plain piece of paper to the other.
The portfolio is now complete.

Cut out the paper on which you will print the flowers or leaves so it has a large enough margin to turn in and glue. Print your design before you attach it to the album; then glue the edges to the chipboard.

Cover the left inside cover with a sheet of plain paper. Attach a pocket on the right inside cover to hold stationery, envelopes, stamps and pens. To make the pocket, cut a sheet of plain paper in the shape shown in Illus. 44, and score it along the dotted lines. Fold the sides of the pocket over and glue them in place. Glue the back of the pocket to the inside of the cover. There is room in the pocket for all your stationery, but no chance of the pocket coming loose from the inside cover.

Illus. 40. Choose flowers and leaves for printing that have prominent veins and other markings. Print on any type of paper—different papers give different effects.

A colorful assortment of pressed flowers can be used to decorate innumerable projects.

A

Because there is no three-dimensionality in pressed flowers, colors seem more vibrant.

B

Flowers and Leaves as Photographic Stencils

To decorate cards and papers with an exact outline of a flower, you can use a photographic process. Since anyone who has the equipment for photography developing—darkroom, developer, photographic paper—probably already knows how to use photographic stencils, the instructions here are intentionally very general.

If you are improvising a darkroom, replace the ordinary electric light bulb with a darkroom bulb (usually a low-watt bulb painted red). This allows you enough light to work by without exposing the photographic paper. Over the work-table should be a source of strong light, at least 5′ above the table so it casts an even intensity of light.

Place the pressed flowers on the photo-sensitive paper and turn the light on for a pre-determined length of time. (The most reliable way to determine the necessary time is to experiment, using the same light the same distance from the table every time, and changing the exposure time until you are satisfied.) When the paper has been ex-

darkroom light

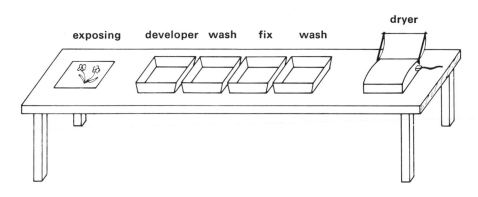

Illus. 41. While a real darkroom is a little more complex than this, the arrangement of steps is the same as the picture shows.

Illus. 42. Greeting cards and stationery can be made in unlimited quantities by making a photographic stencil from a pressed flower.

Illus. 43. A dryer, diagrammed in Illus. 41, presses and dries developed pictures so they lie flat.

posed long enough, turn the light off. Dip the paper evenly into the pan containing the developer (purchased at a photography store). Move the paper back and forth so the developer reaches all areas. Rinse the paper in clear water in the next pan. Now place the paper in the fix bath, and leave it there for about 10 minutes. The paper—which now has the outline of the flower on it—goes into a last wash for about 25 minutes, to remove all chemicals. The paper is finally dried and pressed flat.

As you work with photographic supplies, and as you read the manufacturers' instructions, you will become aware of some safety precautions. For emphasis, though, a few of the most important are mentioned here. Wash your hands

Illus. 44. Pressed flowers make striking pictures in black and white when they are made into photographic films.

thoroughly as you work to prevent chemicals from mixing. Touch the photo-sensitive paper only at the corners, and only with dry hands, so you do not leave fingerprints on it. Unwrap the paper with only the darkroom light on, and never take more than one sheet at a time from the wrappings. Close the package carefully to protect the paper from light.

39

If you plan to use the exposed paper as a greeting card or place card, cover up those parts that you will want to write on later. The photo-sensitive paper is white, but after being exposed and developed it turns black. Illus. 42 to 45 show some designs which were photographically reproduced.

Illus. 45. If you make a photographic stencil, choose flowers and leaves with interesting outlines.

Embedding Plants in Polyester Resin

The projects you have made up until now have all used dried flowers against a flat background. Dried flowers, however, even though they are pressed, still have three dimensions, and the best way to show them off is by embedding the flowers in a clear form. Polyester resin is ideal for this project. It comes in two parts in separate containers, and when mixed in the proper proportions, hardens to as durable a finish as glass.

After you press the flowers for a polyester resin project, brighten their colors with water colors as you do whenever a flower is pale. For this project, though, the flowers must also be coated with varnish or lacquer. If you do not coat them, they will disintegrate and the colors will run as the resin hardens. Be sure that every tiny crevice of the flowers is covered.

While the lacquer dries on the flowers, prepare

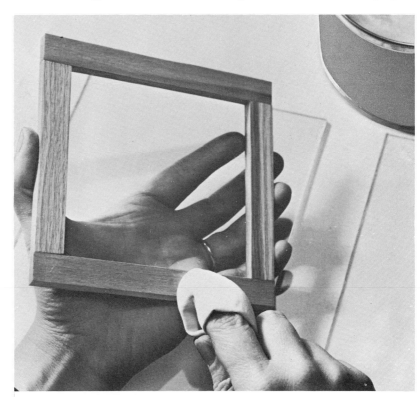

Illus. 46. Make a small wood frame as a mould for the polyester resin. Smooth and sand it before pouring the resin in.

41

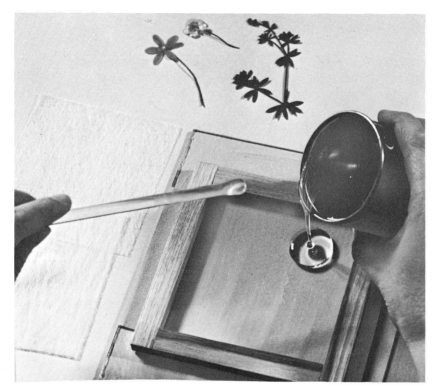

a mould to pour the resin in. The mould can be of glass, wood, steel, metal, or plaster of Paris. Many ready-made moulds for polyester resin are available in craft and hobby shops, in a variety of shapes and sizes, but you can easily make your own. Smooth thin strips of wood moulding with fine sandpaper and glue them together, in a square or whatever shape you desire. (To curve the wood strips, soak them in water until they are pliable; then bend and glue them in the desired shape.)

To be sure that the hardened resin slips easily out of the mould, coat the inside of the mould with a removal agent before you pour the resin. Common removal agents are floor polish or beeswax. They do not stick to the hardened resin. Moulds made of plastics like polyethylene and polypropylene do not need removal agents, since the resin does not stick to them.

While plastic moulds are easiest to use because they require no removal agent, some plastics are dissolved by the liquid resin. To test your mould, put a drop of resin on its surface. After 10 minutes, wipe it away. If the plastic has turned rough or sticky, do not use the mould.

Try lining a small mould that is not plastic with cellophane tape. This sometimes eliminates the need for a removal agent on the inside of the mould.

The ratio of hardening agent to resin depends on the particular brand you are using, but is usually 1 to 10 parts hardening agent to 100 parts resin. For best results, follow the directions on the packages *exactly*. Use a plastic bowl to mix the solution in, and a plastic or wooden spoon for stirring. The resin does not stick to plastic, and can be washed off before it hardens. Once the resin has hardened, it is virtually impossible to remove it from anything.

After mixing the resin and hardening agent, let it stand for a few minutes so air bubbles can escape. With everything at hand—pressed flowers, a clean rag and acetone for cleaning spills—pour about $\frac{1}{2}''$ of the mixture into the mould. As the

Illus. 48. Lay the flowers on top of the resin and gently poke them to release trapped air bubbles.

mixture hardens, it gives off heat; a greater amount of resin produces enough heat to crack the clear material. Even if your mould is very deep, only pour $\frac{1}{2}''$ of resin in at a time.

When you reach the level where you want the flowers, allow the resin to harden only slightly. Place the flowers, leaves and grass on top of this layer. To be sure that no air bubbles remain under the plants, gently prod them with a toothpick.

After this layer has hardened more, mix more resin to fill up the mould. To avoid air bubbles when you add this layer, pour the mixture only into one corner of the mould. The resin will spread forward to fill and surround the plants. Thus, no air bubbles will be formed.

Leave the resin to set at least overnight, but remove it no later than 24 hours after pouring it, to prevent its sticking to the mould. If you lined

Illus. 49. To add a sheet of fibreglass, start at one corner and smoothly press the sheet into the resin.

the mould with enough removal agent, it should easily separate from the hardened form.

While the resin dries, it sometimes rises slightly along the edges of the mould. The surface may be slightly tacky, even when the resin is hard. Polish the resin smooth, beginning with a coarse grade of sandpaper, using finer and finer sandpaper, and finally finishing with a polishing paste used for metal. Use a soft flannel rag for this. Such careful polishing helps make the moulded resin completely transparent, so the most delicate details of the plants are visible.

If you are casting a large, flat piece of polyester resin, add extra strength by placing a sheet of fibreglass on the bottom of the mould. This backing provides a beautifully patterned background for the flowers. First pour a thin layer of resin into the bottom of the mould. Place the fibreglass sheet into the resin, beginning with one corner. Gently push the rest of the fibreglass under the resin with a stiff brush. Pour more resin into the mould, allow it to harden slightly and place the pressed and lacquered flowers on this layer. Add the rest of the resin as you did for a project without a fibreglass base, and then polish the hardened resin until it shines.

There are some synthetic resins just beginning to appear in craft and hobby shops that have certain advantages over the traditional kind: they are non-toxic, non-flammable, and can be used for casting in moulds as above or, when slightly hardened, for sculpting. Treat flowers that are to be embedded in synthetic resin the same way as for polyester resin: first press thoroughly, then coat with lacquer.

Illus. 50. A fibreglass sheet shows up as a beautiful background in a clear resin project.

45

Illus. 51. Pansies suspended in clear polyester resin can be viewed from all sides. Set a piece like this in a sunny spot and let the light shine through it.

Now that you have seen what can be done with pressed flowers, besides pasting them in a scrapbook, look around you to see what else can be decorated. Experiment with place mats with real pressed flowers between two thick plastic sheets, or cloth mats with printed designs in permanent dye. Try covers for boxes, wallpaper patterns, bookmarks, bookplates. Just look around your house, see where flowers might enhance it, and create your own decorations. Use the techniques in this book to attach them.

Illus. 52. Use polyester resin casts in practical projects, too—as a paperweight, bookend or straight edge.

Index

album cover 31–33

book cover 17
book ends 24–25

canister, lacquered 25
centers thicker than petals 6
coasters 16
collector's press 5
coloring flowers 6–8
cutting plants 4

embedding in polyester resin 41–47
eyeglass case 15–16

fibreglass backing in polyester resin 44–45

gathering plants 4
glass 9–14
greeting cards 19–20

hinges for hanging 10–11
holder, napkin 20–22

jewelry 26–27

lacquer as glue 24–30
lamp shade
    curved 17–19
    round, fibreglass 27–29

matchbox cover 22–23
mats 16

napkin holder 20–22

painting flowers 6–8
paper napkin holder 20–22
paper reinforcement 7–8
photo album cover 31–33
photographic stencils 37–40
place cards 19
place mats 16
plants under glass 9–14

plastic film 15–23
polyester resin 41–47
preserving colors 6–8
press, collector's 5
pressing flowers 5–6
printing with plants 31–36

removal agents 42

serving cart 11–12
serving trays 13–14
stationery 19–20

table top 11–12
thick centers 6
trays 13–14

wall decoration 9–10, 25–26
water colors 6–8
wood box, lacquered 30
writing paper 19–20
writing portfolio 34–35